salad

from classics to contemporary

THE AUSTRALIAN
Women's Weekly

contents

AUSTRALIAN CUP AND
SPOON MEASUREMENTS
ARE METRIC.
A CONVERSION CHART
APPEARS ON PAGE 77.

Well haven't salads come a long way.
They were once a boring side-dish made
up of shredded iceberg lettuce, tomato and
cucumber, and if you were lucky a dollop
of store-bought mayonnaise. Today, they are
a delicious meal in their own right. Serve
them chilled or at room temperature; they are
the perfect healthy meal all year round.

Pamela Clark

Food Director

classic salads

GREEK SALAD

prep time 20 minutes **serves** 4
nutritional count per serving 25.8g total fat (9.6g saturated fat);
1359kJ (325 cal); 10.8g carbohydrate; 11.5g protein; 3.2g fibre

¼ cup (60ml) olive oil
1 tablespoon lemon juice
1 tablespoon white wine vinegar
1 tablespoon finely chopped fresh oregano
1 clove garlic, crushed
3 medium tomatoes (450g), cut into wedges
2 lebanese cucumbers (260g),
   chopped coarsely
1 small red onion (100g), sliced thinly
1 small red capsicum (bell pepper) (150g),
   sliced thinly
½ cup (75g) seeded black olives
200g (6½ ounces) fetta cheese,
   chopped coarsely

1 Whisk oil, juice, vinegar, oregano and garlic in large bowl; add remaining ingredients, mix gently.

CAESAR SALAD

prep + cook time 50 minutes **serves** 4
nutritional count per serving 38.4g total fat (9g saturated fat);
2195kJ (525 cal); 28g carbohydrate; 17.7g protein; 4.6g fibre

½ loaf ciabatta bread (220g)
1 clove garlic, crushed
⅓ cup (80ml) olive oil
2 eggs
3 baby cos (romaine) lettuce (540g),
    leaves separated
1 cup (80g) flaked parmesan cheese
caesar dressing
1 clove garlic, crushed
1 tablespoon dijon mustard
2 tablespoons lemon juice
2 teaspoons worcestershire sauce
2 tablespoons olive oil

1 Preheat oven to 180°C/350°F.

2 To make croûtons, cut bread into 2cm (¾-inch) cubes. Combine garlic and oil in large bowl; add bread, toss to coat in mixture. Place bread, in single layer, on oven trays; toast about 15 minutes or until croûtons are browned lightly.

3 Bring water to the boil in small saucepan; using slotted spoon, carefully lower whole unshelled eggs into water. Cover pan tightly, remove from heat; using slotted spoon, remove eggs from water after 1 minute. When cool enough to handle, break eggs into large bowl, add lettuce; toss gently to combine. Add cheese and croûtons.

4 Make caesar dressing. Pour dressing over salad; toss gently to combine. Divide among serving plates; sprinkle with freshly ground black pepper.

caesar dressing Combine ingredients in screw-top jar; shake well.

TABBOULEH

prep time 30 minutes (+ refrigeration) **serves** 4
nutritional count per serving 14.2g total fat (2g saturated fat);
790kJ (189 cal); 9.4g carbohydrate; 3.6g protein; 5.9g fibre

¼ cup (40g) burghul
3 medium tomatoes (450g)
3 cups coarsely chopped fresh
   flat-leaf parsley
3 green onions (scallions), chopped finely
½ cup coarsely chopped fresh mint
1 clove garlic, crushed
¼ cup (60ml) lemon juice
¼ cup (60ml) olive oil

1 Place burghul in shallow medium bowl.
Halve tomatoes, scoop pulp from tomato
over burghul. Chop tomato flesh finely;
spread over burghul. Cover; refrigerate
1 hour.
2 Combine burghul mixture in large bowl
with remaining ingredients.
tips Perfect tabbouleh relies on perfect
parsley: it's imperative that the parsley is
well washed to remove any grit and dried
thoroughly before adding to the salad.
If the parsley is too wet, the tabbouleh
turns a little mushy rather than being light
and tasty. Serve the tabbouleh with
good-quality felafel.

PANZANELLA

prep time 20 minutes **serves** 4
nutritional count per serving 11g total fat (1.5g saturated fat);
1104kJ (264 cal); 33.2g carbohydrate; 7.5g protein; 6g fibre

1 litre (4 cups) water
250g (8 ounces) stale sourdough bread,
   cut into 2cm (¾-inch) slices
2 large tomatoes (440g), chopped coarsely
1 small red onion (100g), sliced thinly
2 lebanese cucumbers (260g),
   chopped coarsely
1 cup firmly packed fresh basil leaves
2 tablespoons olive oil
2 tablespoons red wine vinegar
1 clove garlic, crushed

1 Place the water in large shallow bowl; briefly dip bread slices into water. Pat dry with absorbent paper; tear bread into large chunks.

2 Place bread in large bowl with remaining ingredients; toss gently.

CAPRESE SALAD

prep time 15 minutes **serves** 4
nutritional count per serving 20.6g total fat (8.8g saturated fat);
1028kJ (246 cal); 1.6g carbohydrate; 13.6g protein; 1.1g fibre

3 large egg (plum) tomatoes (270g),
 sliced thinly
300g (9½ ounces) bocconcini cheese,
 drained, sliced thinly
2 tablespoons olive oil
¼ cup firmly packed fresh basil leaves, torn

1 Overlap slices of tomato and cheese on
serving platter.
2 Drizzle with oil; sprinkle with basil.

COLESLAW

prep time 10 minutes **serves** 6
nutritional count per serving 8.1g total fat (1g saturated fat);
523kJ (125 cal); 8.8g carbohydrate; 2g protein; 4.5g fibre

½ small cabbage (600g), shredded finely
1 medium carrot (120g), grated coarsely
4 green onions (scallions), sliced thinly
½ cup (150g) mayonnaise
1 tablespoon lemon juice

1 Combine ingredients in large bowl.

POTATO SALAD

prep + cook time 45 minutes (+ refrigeration) **serves** 8
nutritional count per serving 30.4g total fat (4.1g saturated fat);
1764kJ (422 cal); 29g carbohydrate; 6.2g protein; 3.7g fibre

2kg (4 pounds) potatoes, peeled
2 tablespoons cider vinegar
1 cup (300g) mayonnaise
4 green onions (scallions), sliced thinly
¼ cup finely chopped fresh flat-leaf parsley

1 Cover potatoes with cold water in large saucepan; bring to the boil. Reduce heat; simmer, covered, until tender. Drain; cut into 3cm (1¼-inch) pieces. Spread potato on a tray, sprinkle with vinegar; refrigerate until cold.
2 Place potato in large bowl with mayonnaise, onion and parsley; toss gently to combine.
tip Properly cooked, any waxy, white-fleshed potato will hold its shape when tossed in a salad.

NICOISE SALAD

prep + cook time 20 minutes **serves** 4
nutritional count per serving 16.9g total fat (3.7g saturated fat);
1522kJ (364 cal); 19.5g carbohydrate; 30.9g protein; 5.2g fibre

200g (6½ ounces) baby green beans, trimmed
2 tablespoons olive oil
1 tablespoon lemon juice
2 tablespoons white wine vinegar
4 medium tomatoes (600g), cut into wedges
4 hard-boiled eggs, quartered
425g (13½ ounces) canned tuna in
   springwater, drained, flaked
½ cup (80g) drained caperberries, rinsed
½ cup (60g) seeded small black olives
¼ cup firmly packed fresh flat-leaf
   parsley leaves
440g (14 ounces) canned drained whole new
   potatoes, rinsed, halved

1 Boil, steam or microwave beans until tender; drain. Rinse under cold water; drain.
2 Whisk oil, juice and vinegar in large bowl; add beans and remaining ingredients, mix gently.

tip The original French *salade niçoise* was created with the finest local produce from Provence – vine-ripened tomatoes, piquant caperberries, tiny, firm black olives, hand-picked baby beans and good-quality canned tuna. Our version has adapted a modern approach more suitable to our hectic lifestyle.

FATTOUSH

prep + cook time 20 minutes **serves** 4
nutritional count per serving 19.7g total fat (2.7g saturated fat);
1367kJ (327 cal); 28.1g carbohydrate; 6.8g protein; 5.8g fibre

2 large pitta bread (160g)
⅓ cup (80ml) olive oil
2 tablespoons lemon juice
1 clove garlic, crushed
3 red radishes (105g), trimmed, sliced thinly
½ small daikon (200g), grated coarsely
2 medium tomatoes (300g),
    chopped coarsely
1 lebanese cucumber (130g),
    chopped coarsely
1 small red onion (100g), sliced thinly
1 small green capsicum (bell pepper) (150g),
    chopped coarsely
1 cup loosely packed fresh mint leaves
1 cup loosely packed fresh flat-leaf
    parsley leaves

1 Preheat grill (broiler).
2 Place bread on oven tray; grill until crisp.
Break bread into pieces.
3 Whisk oil, juice and garlic in large bowl.
Mix in half the bread. Add remaining
ingredients; toss gently.
4 Serve fattoush sprinkled with remaining
bread pieces.

WALDORF SALAD

prep time 20 minutes **serves** 4
nutritional count per serving 35.7g total fat (3.1g saturated fat);
1852kJ (443 cal); 22.4g carbohydrate; 5.8g protein; 6.3g fibre

¾ cup (225g) mayonnaise
¼ cup (60ml) lemon juice
5 celery sticks (750g), trimmed, sliced thickly
2 medium red apples (300g), sliced thinly
1 small red onion (100g), sliced thinly
1 cup (100g) roasted walnuts
1 cup loosely packed fresh flat-leaf
   parsley leaves

1 Combine mayonnaise and juice in large bowl; mix in remaining ingredients.

chicken salads

SMOKED CHICKEN AND PEACH SALAD

prep + cook time 20 minutes **serves** 4
nutritional count per serving 50.5g total fat (6.9g saturated fat);
2750kJ (658 cal); 7.4g carbohydrate; 42.4g protein; 5.2g fibre

170g (5½ ounces) asparagus, trimmed,
   cut into 3cm (1¼-inch) lengths
600g (1¼ pounds) smoked chicken breast
   fillets, sliced thinly
1 small red onion (100g), sliced thinly
2 medium peaches (300g), sliced thinly
1 cup (120g) roasted pecans
150g (4½ ounces) baby spinach leaves
dill vinaigrette
⅓ cup (80ml) olive oil
2 tablespoons cider vinegar
1 tablespoon finely chopped fresh dill

1 Boil, steam or microwave asparagus until
tender; drain. Rinse under cold water; drain.
2 Make dill vinaigrette.
3 Place asparagus and vinaigrette with
remaining ingredients in large bowl; toss
gently to combine.
dill vinaigrette Place ingredients in
screw-top jar; shake well.

SESAME CHICKEN
AND HONEY SOY DRESSING

prep + cook time 25 minutes **serves** 4
nutritional count per serving 45.9g total fat (8g saturated fat);
2638kJ (631 cal); 11.8g carbohydrate; 42.1g protein; 3.8g fibre

600g (1¼ pounds) chicken breast fillets,
   halved lengthways
1 egg white, beaten lightly
½ cup (75g) sesame seeds
2 tablespoons olive oil
100g (3 ounces) mixed baby asian greens
1 small red onion (100g), sliced thinly
⅔ cup (100g) coarsely chopped roasted
   unsalted cashews
honey soy dressing
¼ cup (60ml) lemon juice
2 tablespoons light soy sauce
1 tablespoon olive oil
2 teaspoons honey
½ teaspoon sesame oil

1 Dip chicken in egg white, then coat in
sesame seeds. Heat oil in large frying pan;
cook chicken until cooked through. Cover
chicken; stand 5 minutes then slice thickly.
2 Meanwhile, make honey soy dressing.
3 Combine greens, onion and nuts in
medium bowl; divide among serving plates,
top with chicken, drizzle with dressing.
honey soy dressing Combine ingredients
in small bowl.

TANDOORI CHICKEN, SPINACH AND MINT SALAD

prep + cook time 35 minutes (+ refrigeration) **serves** 4
nutritional count per serving 12.5g total fat (3.4g saturated fat);
1731kJ (414 cal); 16.4g carbohydrate; 55.1g protein; 6.7g fibre

⅓ cup (100g) tandoori paste
¼ cup (70g) yogurt
800g (1½ pounds) chicken tenderloins
1 tablespoon vegetable oil
8 large uncooked pappadums
150g (4½ ounces) baby spinach leaves
2 lebanese cucumbers (260g), sliced thickly
250g (8 ounces) cherry tomatoes, halved
1 cup firmly packed fresh mint leaves
spiced yogurt
1 clove garlic, crushed
¾ cup (210g) yogurt
1 tablespoon lemon juice
1 teaspoon ground cumin
1 teaspoon ground coriander

1 Combine paste and yogurt in medium bowl with chicken. Cover; refrigerate 3 hours or overnight.
2 Make spiced yogurt.
3 Heat oil in large frying pan; cook chicken, in batches, until cooked through.
4 Microwave 2 pappadums at a time on HIGH (100%) about 30 seconds.
5 Combine chicken in large bowl with spinach, cucumber, tomato and mint. Drizzle with spiced yogurt; serve with pappadums.
spiced yogurt Combine ingredients in small jug.

CHICKEN RICE SALAD

prep + cook time 25 minutes **serves** 4
nutritional count per serving 27.1g total fat (5.2g saturated fat);
2646kJ (633 cal); 59.3g carbohydrate; 36.3g protein; 3.2g fibre

2 cups (500ml) water
4 x 5cm (2-inch) strips lemon rind
600g (1¼ pounds) chicken breast fillets
3 cups cooked wild rice blend
1 cup thinly sliced fresh mint
½ cup (65g) dried cranberries
2 tablespoons finely chopped preserved
  lemon rind
lemon cranberry dressing
⅓ cup (80ml) olive oil
¼ cup (60ml) cranberry juice
2 tablespoons lemon juice
2 teaspoons caster (superfine) sugar
1 tablespoon cranberry sauce

1 Place the water and rind in medium saucepan; bring to the boil. Add chicken; reduce heat. Simmer, covered, about 10 minutes or until chicken is cooked through. Cool chicken in liquid 10 minutes; drain. Slice chicken thinly.
2 Meanwhile, make lemon cranberry dressing.
3 Place chicken and dressing in large bowl with remaining ingredients; toss gently to combine.
lemon cranberry dressing Place ingredients in screw-top jar; shake well.

seafood salads

GARLIC PRAWN AND NOODLE SALAD

prep + cook time 25 minutes **serves** 4
nutritional count per serving 0.9g total fat (0.1g saturated fat);
564kJ (135 cal); 9.2g carbohydrate; 21.3g protein; 1.7g fibre

750g (1½ pounds) uncooked medium
  king prawns (shrimp)
2 cloves garlic, crushed
125g (4 ounces) rice vermicelli
1 medium lemon (140g)
155g (5 ounces) snow peas,
  sliced thinly lengthways
⅓ cup finely chopped fresh mint

1 Shell and devein prawns, leaving tails intact. Combine prawns and garlic in medium bowl. Cook prawns on heated oiled grill plate (or grill or barbecue) until changed in colour.
2 Meanwhile, place vermicelli in medium heatproof bowl, cover with boiling water; stand until vermicelli is tender, drain.
3 Finely grate 2 teaspoons rind from lemon. Squeeze juice from lemon (you'll need 2 tablespoons juice).
4 Combine prawns, noodles, rind, juice, peas and mint in large bowl; season to taste.

TUNA SALAD

prep time 15 minutes **serves** 4
nutritional count per serving 26.1g total fat (4.9g saturated fat);
1492kJ (357 cal); 4.6g carbohydrate; 24.4g protein; 4.9g fibre

¼ cup (60ml) olive oil
2 tablespoons white wine vinegar
1 tablespoon lemon juice
2 teaspoons finely chopped fresh basil
2 teaspoons finely chopped fresh oregano
1 clove garlic, crushed
1 fresh long red chilli, chopped finely
1 medium iceberg lettuce, cut into wedges
425g (13½ ounces) canned tuna in
   springwater, drained, flaked
250g (8 ounces) cherry tomatoes, halved
1 medium avocado (250g), chopped coarsely
1 lebanese cucumber (130g), sliced thinly
1 small red onion (100g), sliced thinly

1 Combine oil, vinegar, juice, herbs, garlic and chilli in screw-top jar; shake well.
2 Place lettuce wedges on serving plate; top with remaining ingredients. Drizzle with dressing.

tips Feel free to choose any vegetables to toss into this salad; capsicum (bell pepper) and radish would taste great. A can of salmon can be substituted for the tuna.

CRAB AND GREEN MANGO SALAD

prep + cook time 20 minutes **serves** 4
nutritional count per serving 1.4g total fat (0.1g saturated fat);
953kJ (228 cal); 37.2g carbohydrate; 14g protein; 3.9g fibre

125g (4 ounces) bean thread noodles
2 green mangoes (700g), cut into matchsticks
300g (9½ ounces) cooked crab meat, flaked
1 small red onion (100g), sliced thinly
100g (3 ounces) baby mizuna leaves
1 cup firmly packed fresh
   coriander (cilantro) leaves
sweet chilli dressing
⅓ cup (80ml) lime juice
2 tablespoons fish sauce
2 tablespoons sweet chilli sauce
1 tablespoon grated palm sugar

1 Place noodles in medium heatproof bowl, cover with boiling water; stand until almost tender, drain. Rinse under cold water; drain.
2 Meanwhile, make sweet chilli dressing.
3 Place noodles and dressing in large bowl with remaining ingredients; toss gently to combine.
sweet chilli dressing Place ingredients in screw-top jar; shake well.

CHAR-GRILLED CHILLI SQUID SALAD

prep + cook time 30 minutes **serves** 4
nutritional count per serving 3.1g total fat (0.8g saturated fat);
1584kJ (379 cal); 48.3g carbohydrate; 38.1g protein; 2.8g fibre

800g (1½ pounds) cleaned squid hoods
450g (14½ ounces) fresh wide rice noodles
1 medium red capsicum (bell pepper) (200g),
   sliced thinly
150g (4½ ounces) snow peas,
   trimmed, halved
1 lebanese cucumber (130g), seeded,
   sliced thinly
1 small red onion (100g), sliced thinly
1 cup loosely packed fresh
   coriander (cilantro) leaves
⅓ cup coarsely chopped fresh mint
sweet chilli dressing
½ cup (125ml) water
⅓ cup (75g) caster (superfine) sugar
1 tablespoon white vinegar
2 fresh small red thai (serrano) chillies,
   chopped finely

1 Cut squid down centre to open out;
score the inside in a diagonal pattern.
Halve squid lengthways; cut squid into
3cm (1¼-inch) pieces.
2 Make sweet chilli dressing.
3 Cook squid on heated oiled grill plate
(or grill or barbecue), in batches, until
tender and browned.
4 Place noodles in large heatproof bowl,
cover with boiling water; separate with
fork, drain. Combine noodles in large
serving bowl with squid, dressing and
remaining ingredients.
sweet chilli dressing Stir the water and
sugar in small saucepan, over low heat,
until sugar dissolves; bring to the boil.
Reduce heat; simmer, uncovered, without
stirring, about 5 minutes or until syrup
thickens slightly. Stir in vinegar and chilli
off the heat.

BARBECUED OCTOPUS SALAD

prep + cook time 25 minutes **serves** 4
nutritional count per serving 1.9g total fat (0g saturated fat);
681kJ (163 cal); 6.9g carbohydrate; 27.4g protein; 3.4g fibre

600g (1¼ pounds) baby octopus
1 teaspoon finely grated lemon rind
2 tablespoons lemon juice
2 teaspoons finely chopped fresh oregano
1 clove garlic, crushed
½ teaspoon cracked black pepper
cooking-oil spray
tomato salad
4 medium tomatoes (600g), seeded,
    chopped coarsely
2 lebanese cucumbers (260g),
    chopped coarsely
1 small red onion (100g), chopped finely
1 small green capsicum (bell pepper) (150g),
    chopped coarsely
1 tablespoon coarsely chopped fresh
    oregano leaves
1 tablespoon white wine vinegar

1 Make tomato salad.
2 Combine octopus, rind, juice, oregano, garlic and pepper in medium bowl.
3 Spray heated barbecue grill plate (or grill or barbecue) with cooking-oil spray for 2 seconds. Cook octopus, turning occasionally, until cooked through.
4 Serve octopus with tomato salad, and lemon wedges, if you like.
tomato salad Toss ingredients gently in medium bowl.

CAJUN FISH SALAD

prep + cook time 25 minutes **serves** 4
nutritional count per serving 5g total fat (1.5g saturated fat);
1070kJ (256 cal); 5.8g carbohydrate; 45g protein; 2.7g fibre

1 tablespoon cajun spice mix
½ teaspoon sea salt flakes
2 x 200g (6½-ounce) firm white fish fillets
cooking-oil spray
2 lebanese cucumbers (260g), seeded,
  sliced thinly
150g (4½ ounces) sugar snap peas, trimmed,
  halved lengthways
100g (3 ounces) baby asian greens
1 cup loosely packed fresh coriander
  (cilantro) leaves
½ cup loosely packed fresh mint leaves
1 green onion (scallion), sliced thinly
yogurt dressing
½ cup (140g) low-fat natural yogurt
2 tablespoons lemon juice

1 Combine spice mix and salt in
medium shallow bowl, add fish; coat in
spice mixture.
2 Spray heated medium frying pan with
cooking-oil; cook fish, over medium heat,
about 5 minutes each side or until cooked
through. Cover; stand 5 minutes. Using two
forks, flake fish into pieces.
3 Meanwhile, make yogurt dressing.
4 Place cucumber, peas, asian greens,
herbs and onion in large bowl; toss gently to
combine. Serve salad topped with flaked
fish; drizzle with dressing.
yogurt dressing Combine ingredients in
small bowl.

meat salads

WARM THAI BEEF SALAD

prep + cook time 30 minutes **serves** 6
nutritional count per serving 10.6g total fat (4.2g saturated fat);
1597kJ (382 cal); 34g carbohydrate; 35.3g protein; 3.4g fibre

800g (1½-pound) piece beef rump steak
1 teaspoon peanut oil
250g (8 ounces) bean thread vermicelli
1 telegraph (hothouse) cucumber (400g),
  halved lengthways, sliced thinly
1 large red capsicum (bell pepper) (350g),
  sliced thinly
1 small red onion (100g), sliced thinly
1 fresh long red chilli, sliced thinly
1 cup firmly packed fresh mint leaves
1 cup firmly packed fresh
  coriander (cilantro) leaves
lime dressing
1 tablespoon coarsely chopped fresh
  coriander (cilantro) root and stem mixture
5 cloves garlic, chopped coarsely
1 teaspoon black peppercorns
½ cup (125ml) lime juice
1 tablespoon fish sauce
1 tablespoon grated palm sugar
2 x 10cm (4-inch) sticks fresh
  lemon grass (40g), chopped coarsely

1 Brush beef, both sides, with oil; cook
on heated grill plate (or grill or barbecue)
until cooked as desired. Cover beef; stand
5 minutes.
2 Place vermicelli in large heatproof bowl,
cover with boiling water; stand until tender,
drain. Cut vermicelli into random lengths
back into same bowl.
3 Meanwhile, make lime dressing.
4 Slice beef thinly; combine in large bowl
with half the dressing and remaining
ingredients. Drizzle remaining dressing over
vermicelli. Divide vermicelli among shallow
serving bowls; top with salad.
lime dressing Blend or process ingredients
until chopped finely.
tip To prepare the coriander (cilantro) root
and stem mixture, wash the coriander under
cold water, removing any dirt clinging to the
roots; scrape the roots with a small flat knife
to remove some of the outer fibrous skin.
Chop the coriander roots and stems
together to obtain the amount specified.

LAMB AND LENTIL SALAD

prep + cook time 40 minutes **serves** 6
nutritional count per serving 41.3g total fat (10.2g saturated fat); 2880kJ (689 cal); 26.4g carbohydrate; 48.3g protein; 10.8g fibre

1½ cups (300g) french-style green lentils
750g (1½ pounds) lamb backstraps
1 tablespoon olive oil
2 teaspoons ground cumin
350g (11 ounces) baby green beans
1 small red onion (100g), sliced thinly
1 cup (110g) coarsely chopped
   roasted walnuts
2 cups firmly packed fresh flat-leaf
   parsley leaves
200g (6½ ounces) fetta cheese, crumbled
pomegranate dressing
⅓ cup (80ml) olive oil
2 tablespoons lemon juice
1 tablespoon pomegranate molasses
2 teaspoons light brown sugar

1 Cook lentils in large saucepan of boiling water, uncovered, about 15 minutes or until tender; drain.

2 Meanwhile, make pomegranate dressing.

3 Combine half the dressing with lentils in large bowl.

4 Cook lamb on heated oiled grill plate (or grill or barbecue), brushing frequently with combined oil and cumin, until cooked as desired. Cover lamb; stand 5 minutes then slice thickly.

5 Boil, steam or microwave beans until tender; drain. Rinse under cold water; drain.

6 Add onion, nuts, parsley, cheese and remaining dressing to lentils; toss gently to combine. Serve lentil mixture topped with beans and lamb.

pomegranate dressing Combine ingredients in screw-top jar; shake well.

tip Pomegranate molasses is available at Middle-Eastern food stores, specialty-food shops and some delicatessens.

PORK AND BEETROOT SALAD

prep + cook time 50 minutes **serves** 6
nutritional count per serving 33.2g total fat (10.6g saturated fat);
2249kJ (538 cal); 20.5g carbohydrate; 35.8g protein; 8.8g fibre

2 bunches baby beetroot (beets) (1kg)
2 bunches spring onions (800g)
2 tablespoons olive oil
750g (1½ pounds) pork fillets
150g (4½ ounces) mixed baby asian greens
1 cup (100g) coarsely chopped
   roasted walnuts
horseradish dressing
¾ cup (180g) crème fraîche
3 teaspoons dijon mustard
3 teaspoons prepared horseradish
1 tablespoon lemon juice
2 tablespoons water

1 Preheat oven to 200°C/400°F.
2 Trim stalk and root ends of beetroot to
make 3cm (1¼-inch) lengths; halve beetroot
lengthways. Trim roots from onions; trim
stems to make 5cm (2-inch) lengths. Halve
onions lengthways. Place beetroot and
onion, in single layer, in large shallow baking
dish; drizzle with half the oil. Roast,
uncovered, 30 minutes or until tender.
3 Meanwhile, heat remaining oil in large
frying pan; cook pork until cooked as
desired. Cover pork; stand 5 minutes then
slice thickly.
4 Make horseradish dressing.
5 Divide asian greens among serving plates;
top with roasted vegetables and sliced pork.
Drizzle with dressing; sprinkle with nuts.
horseradish dressing Whisk ingredients in
small bowl until smooth.

MEXICAN BEEF SALAD

prep + cook time 15 minutes **serves** 4
nutritional count per serving 10.7g total fat (4.6g saturated fat);
1392kJ (333 cal); 15.9g carbohydrate; 39.8g protein; 6.6g fibre

35g (1 ounce) packet taco seasoning mix
600g (1¼-pound) piece beef rump steak
420g (13½ ounces) canned four-bean mix,
    rinsed, drained
125g (4 ounces) canned corn kernels,
    rinsed, drained
2 large tomatoes (440g), chopped finely
½ cup coarsely chopped
    fresh coriander (cilantro)

1 Rub seasoning mix over both sides of
steak. Cook steak in heated oiled large
frying pan. Cover steak; stand 5 minutes;
slice thickly.
2 Meanwhile, combine beans, corn, tomato
and coriander in medium bowl. Divide salad
between serving plates; top with steak.
Serve with lime wedges, if you like.

PEPPERED LAMB AND WATERCRESS

prep + cook time 30 minutes **serves** 4
nutritional count per serving 31.1g total fat (12g saturated fat);
2006kJ (480 cal); 5.1g carbohydrate; 43.2g protein; 5g fibre

2 tablespoons mixed peppercorns
1 tablespoon olive oil
600g (1¼ pounds) lamb fillets
1 cup (160g) fresh or frozen peas
250g (8 ounces) yellow teardrop
   tomatoes, halved
1 cup (115g) firmly packed
   trimmed watercress
200g (6½ ounces) fetta cheese,
   cut into thin strips
¼ cup coarsely chopped fresh mint
white wine vinaigrette
¼ cup (60ml) white wine vinegar
1 tablespoon olive oil
1 clove garlic, crushed

1 Using mortar and pestle, crush peppercorns until ground coarsely. Combine ground peppercorns, oil and lamb in medium bowl.
2 Cook lamb in heated oiled large frying pan until cooked as desired. Cover lamb; stand 5 minutes; slice thinly.
3 Meanwhile, make white wine vinaigrette.
4 Boil, steam or microwave peas until tender; drain. Rinse under cold water; drain.
5 Place lamb, peas and vinaigrette in large bowl with remaining ingredients; toss gently to combine.

white wine vinaigrette Place ingredients in screw-top jar; shake well.

SPICY PORK AND APPLE SALAD

prep + cook time 15 minutes **serves** 4
nutritional count per serving 2.6g total fat (0.7g saturated fat);
631kJ (151 cal); 9.4g carbohydrate; 20.6g protein; 3.6g fibre

350g (11 ounces) pork fillet
2 tablespoons lime juice
1 tablespoon finely chopped fresh oregano
2 cloves garlic, crushed
1 teaspoon ground cumin
cooking-oil spray
2 cups (230g) firmly packed
   trimmed watercress
2 medium apples (300g), sliced thickly
250g (8 ounces) red grape tomatoes, halved
2 tablespoons finely chopped fresh mint

1 Combine pork, juice, oregano, garlic and cumin in medium bowl.
2 Spray heated medium frying pan with cooking-oil; cook pork until browned all over and cooked through. Cover; stand 10 minutes then slice pork thinly.
3 Place pork in large bowl with watercress, apple, tomatoes and mint. Serve with lime wedges, if you like.

vegetable, grain & egg salads

GADO GADO

prep + cook time 45 minutes **serves** 4
nutritional count per serving 9.8g total fat (8.8g saturated fat);
1208kJ (289 cal); 20.3g carbohydrate; 11.1g protein; 9.2g fibre

4 medium carrots (480g), cut into batons
1 medium potato (200g), chopped coarsely
200g (6½ ounces) cauliflower, cut into florets
100g (3 ounces) snow peas, trimmed, halved
1 lebanese cucumber (130g), cut into batons
1½ cups (100g) coarsely chopped
  iceberg lettuce
1½ cups (120g) bean sprouts
½ cup coarsely chopped fresh
  coriander (cilantro)
peanut sauce
½ cup (70g) roasted unsalted peanuts
2 cloves garlic, quartered
4 green onions (scallions), chopped coarsely
½ teaspoon light brown sugar
1 tablespoon soy sauce
½ teaspoon chilli powder
1 tablespoon lemon juice
¾ cup (180ml) water
⅔ cup (160ml) light coconut milk

1 Boil, steam or microwave carrot, potato, cauliflower and peas, separately, until just tender; drain. Rinse under cold water; drain.
2 Meanwhile, make peanut sauce.
3 Place carrot, potato, cauliflower and peas in large bowl with cucumber, lettuce, sprouts and coriander; toss gently to combine. Serve salad drizzled with peanut sauce.
peanut sauce Using mortar and pestle, grind nuts until crushed finely; transfer to small bowl. Using mortar and pestle, crush garlic and green onion into a coarse paste. Cook garlic mixture in medium lightly oiled frying pan, stirring, 2 minutes. Add remaining ingredients; bring to the boil. Reduce heat; simmer, uncovered, 3 minutes. Add nuts; simmer, uncovered, 5 minutes.

ITALIAN BROWN RICE SALAD

prep + cook time 1 hour 15 minutes **serves** 4
nutritional count per serving 13.3g total fat (1.8g saturated fat);
1923kJ (460 cal); 76.3g carbohydrate; 14.7g protein; 9.4g fibre

3 cups (750ml) vegetable stock
2 teaspoons olive oil
1 small brown onion (80g), chopped finely
1½ cups (300g) brown medium-grain rice
1 teaspoon finely grated lime rind
1 clove garlic, crushed
⅓ cup (45g) roasted slivered almonds
⅔ cup (100g) sun-dried tomatoes,
   chopped coarsely
½ cup (60g) seeded black olives,
   chopped coarsely
½ cup coarsely chopped fresh basil
¼ cup coarsely chopped fresh
   flat-leaf parsley
lime and mustard dressing
2 tablespoons lime juice
2 tablespoons white wine vinegar
2 cloves garlic, crushed
2 teaspoons dijon mustard

1 Place stock in medium saucepan; bring to the boil. Reduce heat; simmer, covered.
2 Meanwhile, heat oil in large saucepan; cook onion, stirring, until soft. Add rice, rind and garlic; stir to coat rice in onion mixture.
3 Add stock; bring to the boil. Reduce heat; simmer, covered, about 50 minutes or until rice is tender and liquid is absorbed.
4 Make lime and mustard dressing.
5 Add nuts, tomato, olives, basil and dressing to rice mixture in pan; toss gently to combine.
6 Serve salad warm; top with parsley.
lime and mustard dressing Combine ingredients in screw-top jar; shake well.
tip We used the sun-dried tomatoes that have not been preserved in oil; they are generally sold in plastic bags or loose by weight.

MOROCCAN COUSCOUS SALAD

prep time 20 minutes **serves** 4
nutritional count per serving 29g total fat (5.5g saturated fat);
268kJ (686 cal); 85.6g carbohydrate; 17.2g protein; 6.5g fibre

1½ cups (300g) couscous
1½ cups (375ml) boiling water
20g (¾ ounce) butter
420g (13½ ounces) canned chickpeas
    (garbanzo beans), rinsed, drained
⅓ cup (55g) sultanas
⅓ cup (50g) roasted pine nuts
100g (3 ounces) baby rocket leaves (arugula),
    chopped coarsely
¾ cup finely chopped fresh flat-leaf parsley
1 cup (120g) seeded green olives
preserved lemon dressing
1 tablespoon finely grated lemon rind
¼ cup (60ml) lemon juice
¼ cup (60ml) olive oil
2 tablespoons finely chopped preserved
    lemon rind

1 Combine couscous with the water in
large heatproof bowl, cover; stand about
5 minutes or until liquid is absorbed, fluffing
with fork occasionally. Stir in butter; stand
10 minutes.
2 Make preserved lemon dressing.
3 Combine couscous in large bowl with
remaining ingredients and dressing.
preserved lemon dressing Combine
ingredients in screw-top jar; shake well.
tip Preserved lemon is a North African
speciality, where lemons, whole or sliced,
are placed in a mixture of salt and oil or
lemon juice. To use, remove and discard
pulp, squeeze juice from rind; rinse rind well,
then slice it thinly.

PUMPKIN RAVIOLI
AND ROASTED TOMATO SALAD

prep + cook time 30 minutes **serves** 6
nutritional count per serving 18g total fat (4.7g saturated fat); 1542kJ (369 cal); 35g carbohydrate; 14.3g protein; 5.2g fibre

500g (1 pound) cherry tomatoes, halved
2 medium red onions (340g), halved,
   sliced thinly
1 teaspoon caster (superfine) sugar
¼ cup (60ml) olive oil
1kg (2 pounds) pumpkin ravioli
100g (3 ounces) baby rocket leaves (arugula)
150g (4½ ounces) small black olives, seeded
2 tablespoons rinsed, drained baby capers
2 tablespoons red wine vinegar

1 Preheat oven to 220°C/425°F. Line oven tray with baking paper.
2 Place tomato and onion on tray in a single layer; sprinkle with sugar, drizzle with 1 tablespoon of the oil. Roast, uncovered, about 20 minutes.
3 Meanwhile, cook ravioli in large saucepan of boiling water until tender; drain.
4 Combine ravioli in large bowl with tomato, onion, rocket, olives and capers.
5 Dress salad with combined vinegar and remaining oil.

HALOUMI AND POMEGRANATE SALAD

prep + cook time 20 minutes **serves** 4
nutritional count per serving 24.7g total fat (11.2g saturated fat);
1400kJ (335 cal); 6.5g carbohydrate; 20.6g protein; 3.5g fibre

1 tablespoon lemon juice
2 tablespoons light olive oil
⅓ cup (80ml) pomegranate pulp
¼ cup firmly packed fresh mint leaves
2 green onions (scallions), sliced thinly
125g (4 ounces) mizuna
1 medium fennel (300g), trimmed,
   sliced thinly
360g (11½ ounces) haloumi cheese,
   sliced thickly

1 Combine juice, oil, pulp, mint, onion,
mizuna and fennel in large bowl.
2 Heat large oiled frying pan, cook cheese
until browned both sides. Serve salad
topped with cheese.

CURRIED EGG SALAD

prep time 20 minutes **serves** 4
nutritional count per serving 15.2g total fat (3g saturated fat);
832kJ (199 cal); 6.1g carbohydrate; 9.3g protein; 1.2g fibre

1 celery stick (150g), trimmed,
   cut into matchsticks
¼ small red onion (25g), sliced thinly
½ cup coarsely chopped fresh
   flat-leaf parsley
4 hard-boiled eggs, grated finely
4 small butter (boston) lettuce
   leaves, chopped
curry mayonnaise
⅓ cup (100g) mayonnaise
1 tablespoon lemon juice
½ teaspoon curry powder

1 Make curry mayonnaise.
2 Combine celery, onion and parsley in
medium bowl.
3 Spread lettuce on serving plates,
top with egg then celery mixture; drizzle
with mayonnaise.
curry mayonnaise Combine ingredients in
small bowl.

COS LETTUCE

This is a robust lettuce with a crisp spine and neutral-tasting leaves that stand up well to heavy dressings and other substantial ingredients such as eggs, fish or bacon. Regular cos (above) have a lot of leaf wastage because the outside leaves are tough and coarse, but baby cos have little wastage. Both are available all year. It's also known as romaine.

RADICCHIO

This sturdy chicory comes in numerous varieties, some with red and green leaves, and some with red and white leaves. The different kinds are often called after their places of origin, such as round-headed verona and elongated treviso. Its robust, bitter leaves can also be used for braising or barbecuing. It is available all year but is best in winter.

BABY SPINACH LEAVES

These taste much like mature spinach, having a delicate, earthy flavour, but are a little less tart. Both the stems and leaves are eaten, so choose undamaged, dark green, firm leaves and crisp stems. The leaves are perishable, so eat them soon after buying. Spinach is available all year round, but is at its peak in cooler winter months.

MESCLUN

Also known as salad mix or gourmet salad mix, mesclun is a mix of assorted young lettuce and other baby green leaves, including baby spinach leaves, mizuna and curly endive. Mesclun is available all year round from supermarkets, usually packaged, or in loose form from greengrocers.

SALAD GREENS

ROCKET

Is available both wild and cultivated and also as very young or baby rocket. Its flavour has been described as roast beef with a peppery tang. Wild rocket is the hottest, cultivated rocket is less peppery because it is grown more quickly and baby rocket is the mildest. Is also known as roquette, rugula, arugula and rucola. Rocket is available all year.

MIZUNA

Also called mitsuba, this leafy Japanese herb has a crisp, aromatic flavour. Its sharply jagged leaves are similar in size and shape to baby rocket leaves, and have a mild-mustard taste, which is highlighted when paired with a miso-based or japanese-flavoured dressing. Its peak season is summer but it is available most of the year.

ICEBERG LETTUCE

A crisp, refreshing lettuce with a watery crunch. Best eaten when absolutely fresh, iceberg has a very simple taste, allowing it to mix well with a great variety of flavours and textures. Use in a simple crunchy salad or with hard-boiled eggs in a sandwich. Iceberg is available all year.

OAKLEAF LETTUCE

These are mildly flavoured with loose, soft, ruffled, floppy green (above) or red-flushed leaves that look lovely with other leaves in a tossed salad. It is often described as a cut-and-come-again lettuce because, if you grow your own, you can take leaves as you need them without affecting the plant. It is available all year.

CLASSIC FRENCH

prep time 5 minutes
makes about 1 cup (250ml)
nutritional count per tablespoon 13.7g total fat
(1.9g saturated fat); 506kJ (121 cal);
0.2g carbohydrate; 0g protein; 0g fibre

Place ¼ cup white vinegar, ¾ cup olive oil,
½ teaspoon caster (superfine) sugar and
1 teaspoon dijon mustard in screw-top jar;
shake well.

CLASSIC ITALIAN

prep time 10 minutes
makes about 1 cup (250ml)
nutritional count per tablespoon 13.7g total fat
(1.9g saturated fat); 510kJ (122 cal);
0.3g carbohydrate; 0.1g protein; 0.1g fibre

Place 2 tablespoons white wine vinegar,
2 tablespoons lemon juice, ½ teaspoon
caster (superfine) sugar, 2 cloves crushed
garlic, ¾ cup olive oil, 1 tablespoon finely
chopped fresh basil leaves and 1 tablespoon
finely chopped fresh oregano leaves in
screw-top jar; shake well.

SALAD DRESSINGS

THOUSAND ISLAND

prep time 10 minutes
makes 1 cup (250ml)
nutritional count per tablespoon 4.3g total fat
(0.5g saturated fat); 226kJ (54 cal);
3.6g carbohydrate; 0.3g protein; 0.4g fibre

Combine ½ cup mayonnaise,
1½ tablespoons tomato sauce (ketchup),
½ finely grated small white onion, 8 finely
chopped pimiento-stuffed green olives
and ½ finely chopped small red capsicum
(bell pepper) in small bowl.

CLASSIC MAYONNAISE

prep time 15 minutes
makes 1 cup (250ml)
nutritional count per tablespoon 19.2g total fat
(2.9g saturated fat); 719kJ (172 cal);
0g carbohydrate; 0.5g protein; 0g fibre

Combine 2 egg yolks, ½ teaspoon coarse
cooking (kosher) salt and 1 teaspoon dijon
mustard in medium bowl. Gradually add
⅔ cup extra light olive oil and ⅓ cup olive
oil in a thin, steady stream, whisking
constantly until mixture thickens. Stir in
1 tablespoon white wine vinegar and
1 tablespoon lemon juice.

GREEN GODDESS

prep time 10 minutes
makes 1¼ cup (310ml)
nutritional count per tablespoon 24.2g total fat
(2.9g saturated fat); 1166kJ (279 cal);
14.6g carbohydrate; 1.2g protein; 0.6g fibre

Combine 1 cup mayonnaise, 2 finely
chopped anchovy fillets, 2 thinly sliced
green onions (scallions), 2 teaspoons finely
chopped fresh flat-leaf parsley, 2 teaspoons
finely chopped fresh chives, 2 teaspoons
finely chopped fresh tarragon and
2 teaspoons cider vinegar in small bowl.

CLASSIC PESTO

prep time 10 minutes
makes 1 cup (250ml)
nutritional count per tablespoon 7.7g total fat
(1.4g saturated fat); 322kJ (77 cal);
0.8g carbohydrate; 1.3g protein; 0.2g fibre

Blend or process 2 crushed garlic cloves,
¼ cup finely grated parmesan cheese,
1 tablespoon roasted pine nuts,
1 tablespoon lemon juice, 1 cup firmly
packed fresh basil leaves and ⅓ cup olive oil
until smooth. Transfer basil mixture to small
bowl; stir in ½ cup buttermilk.

BALSAMIC AND GARLIC

prep time 5 minutes
makes 1¼ cups (310ml)
nutritional count per tablespoon 10.9g total fat
(1.5g saturated fat); 406kJ (97 cal);
0.1g carbohydrate; 0g protein; 0g fibre

Whisk 2 tablespoons balsamic vinegar,
¼ cup lemon juice, 1 crushed garlic
clove and ¾ cup olive oil in small bowl
until combined.

AMERICAN RANCH

prep time 10 minutes
makes 1 cup (250ml)
nutritional count per tablespoon 4.2g total fat
(0.5g saturated fat); 217kJ (52 cal);
3.2g carbohydrate; 0.5g protein; 0.2g fibre

Whisk ½ cup mayonnaise, ¼ cup buttermilk,
1 tablespoon white wine vinegar, 1 finely
chopped small brown onion, 1 crushed
garlic clove, 1 tablespoon finely chopped
fresh chives, 1 tablespoon finely chopped
fresh flat-leaf parsley and ¼ teaspoon sweet
paprika in small jug until combined.

ARTICHOKE HEARTS tender centre of the globe artichoke; purchased in brine canned or in glass jars.

ASIAN GREENS, MIXED BABY mix of baby buk choy, choy sum, gai lan and water spinach. Available from Asian food stores and selected supermarkets.

BACON from cured, smoked pork side.

BAKING PAPER also parchment paper or baking parchment – a silicone-coated paper primarily used for lining baking pans and oven trays so cakes and biscuits won't stick.

BEANS

borlotti also known as roman beans or pink beans, available fresh or dried. Interchangeable with pinto beans because of the similarity in appearance – both are pale pink or beige with dark red streaks.

butter also known as lima beans; large, flat, kidney-shaped bean, off-white in colour, with a mealy texture and mild taste. Available canned and dried.

four-bean mix a mix of kidney, butter and cannellini beans, and chickpeas.

soya low in carbohydrates and high in protein; the source of products such as tofu, soy milk, soy sauce, tamari and miso. Available dried and canned; sometimes sold fresh as edamame.

BEETROOT known as red beets or just beets; firm, round root vegetable.

BREAD

ciabatta in Italian the word means 'slipper', which is the traditional shape of this crisp white bread.

french stick bread that's been formed into a long, narrow, cylindrical loaf. Usually has a crisp brown crust and a light chewy interior. Also known as french bread, french loaf or baguette.

pitta also known as lebanese bread. A wheat-flour pocket bread sold in large, flat pieces that separate into two thin rounds. Also available in small thick pieces called pocket pitta.

sourdough has a slightly sour taste from the yeast starter culture used to make the bread. A low-risen bread with a dense centre and crisp crust.

BREADCRUMBS, PACKAGED fine-textured, crunchy, purchased white breadcrumbs.

BURGHUL made from whole wheat kernels that are steamed, dried and toasted before cracking into several distinct sizes, so they develop a rich, nutty flavour. Because it is already partially cooked, burghul only requires minimal cooking. Cracked wheat, on the other hand, is raw whole wheat.

CAPSICUM also known as bell pepper or, simply, pepper; comes in green, red, yellow, orange and eggplant colours. Discard membranes and seeds before using.

CHAR-GRILLED ANTIPASTO marinated char-grilled vegetables that usually include capsicum, eggplant and zucchini and other vegetables.

CHEESE

blue mould-treated cheeses mottled with blue veining. Varieties include firm and crumbly stilton types to mild, creamy brie-like cheeses.

bocconcini from the diminutive of boccone meaning 'mouthful'; is the term used for walnut-sized, baby mozzarella. A delicate, semi-soft, white cheese traditionally made in Italy from buffalo milk. Spoils rapidly so must be kept under refrigeration, in brine, for 1 or 2 days at most. Cherry bocconcini are even smaller in size.

fetta Greek in origin; a crumbly textured goat- or sheep-milk cheese with a sharp, salty taste.

haloumi a firm, cream-coloured sheep-milk cheese matured in brine. Somewhat like a minty, salty fetta in flavour, haloumi can be grilled or fried, briefly, without breaking down. It should be eaten while still warm as it becomes tough and rubbery on cooling.

parmesan also known as parmigiana; a hard, grainy, cows'-milk cheese that originated in the Parma region of Italy. The curd is salted in brine for a month before being aged for up to two years in humid conditions.

ricotta soft, white, cows'-milk cheese; roughly translates as 'cooked again'. It's made from whey, a by-product of other cheese making, to which fresh milk and acid are added. Ricotta is a sweet, moist cheese with a slightly grainy texture.

CHICKPEAS also called garbanzos, hummus or channa; an irregularly round, sandy-coloured legume.

CHILLI available in many different types and sizes. Use rubber gloves when seeding and chopping fresh chillies as they can burn your skin. Removing seeds and membranes lessens the heat level.

GLOSSARY

flakes dried, deep-red, dehydrated chilli slices and whole seeds.

long red available both fresh and dried; a generic term used for any moderately hot, long, thin chilli (about 6-8cm/2½-3 inches long).

red thai also known as 'scuds'; tiny, hot and bright red in colour.

CHINESE COOKING WINE also known as shao hsing or chinese rice wine. Inexpensive and found in Asian food shops; if you can't find it, replace with mirin or sherry.

CHORIZO SAUSAGES Spanish in origin; made of coarsely ground pork and highly seasoned with garlic and chilli. They are deeply smoked, very spicy and dry-cured. Also available raw.

COUSCOUS a fine, grain-like cereal product made from semolina. A dough of semolina flour and water is sieved then dehydrated to produce minuscule even-sized pellets of couscous; it is rehydrated by steaming, or with the addition of a warm liquid, and swells to three or four times its original size.

CREAM, POURING we used fresh cream, also known as pure or single cream, unless otherwise stated.

CREME FRAICHE mature fermented cream with a slightly tangy, nutty flavour and velvety texture. Can boil without curdling and can be used in both sweet and savoury dishes.

DILL PICKLE a small cucumber that's been preserved in brine or vinegar flavoured with dill seeds.

EGGPLANT, BABY also known as finger or japanese eggplant; very small and slender so can be used without disgorging (salting to remove any bitter juices).

EGGS some recipes in this book call for raw or barely cooked eggs; exercise caution if there's a salmonella problem in your area, particularly in food eaten by children and pregnant women.

FLOUR

plain an all-purpose wheat flour.

rice a very fine flour made from ground white rice.

GINGER also known as green or root ginger; the thick root of a tropical plant. Pickled ginger is sold in pieces or sliced, and comes in red and pink varieties packed in a mixture of vinegar, sugar and natural colouring.

HORSERADISH CREAM a creamy paste made of grated horseradish, vinegar, oil and sugar.

preserved grated horseradish root.

KECAP MANIS see sauces, soy.

KUMARA name of an orange-fleshed sweet potato often confused with yam.

LEEK a member of the onion family; subtle in flavour.

LEMON GRASS a tall, clumping, lemon-smelling and -tasting, sharp-edged grass; the white lower part of each stem is chopped and used in Asian cooking.

LENTILS (RED, BROWN, YELLOW) dried pulses often identified by, and named after, their colour.

french-style green lentils related to the famous french lentils du puy; these green-blue, tiny lentils have a nutty, earthy flavour and a hardy nature that allows them to be rapidly cooked without disintegrating. Also known as australian, bondi or matilda lentils.

LETTUCE see 'Salad Greens' p68.

LYCHEES small fruit from China with a hard shell and sweet, juicy flesh. The white flesh has a gelatinous texture and musky, perfumed taste. Discard the rough skin and seed before using.

PANCETTA an Italian-style bacon; cured but not smoked.

PAPPADUMS sun-dried wafers made from a combination of lentil and rice flours, oil and spices.

PEPITAS edible pumpkin seeds that have had their white hull removed; are green, with a delicate nutty flavour.

PINE NUTS also known as pignoli; not, in fact, a nut, but a small, cream-coloured kernel from pine cones.

POMEGRANATE dark-red, leathery-skinned fruit about the size of an orange filled with hundreds of seeds, each wrapped in an edible lucent-crimson pulp having a tangy sweet-sour flavour.

POMEGRANATE MOLASSES has tart and fruity qualities similar to balsamic vinegar. Is thicker, browner and more concentrated in flavour than grenadine, the sweet, red pomegranate syrup used in cocktails. Available at Middle Eastern food stores, specialty food shops and better delicatessens.

POTATOES, BABY NEW also known as chats; an early harvest with thin skin.

PROSCIUTTO a kind of unsmoked Italian ham; salted, air-cured and aged, it is usually eaten uncooked.

SAKE Japanese wine, made from fermented rice.

SAMBAL OELEK (also ulek or olek) Indonesian; a salty paste made from chillies and vinegar.

SAUCES

cranberry, whole berry made of cranberries cooked in sugar syrup; has an astringent flavour.

fish also called nam pla or nuoc nam; made from pulverised salted fermented fish, most often anchovies. Has a strong taste and pungent smell; use sparingly.

oyster Asian in origin, this rich, brown sauce is made from oysters and their brine, cooked with salt and soy sauce, and thickened with starches.

plum a thick sauce made from plums, vinegar, sugar, chillies and spices.

soy made from fermented soya beans. Several variations are available in most supermarkets and Asian food stores.

dark soy deep brown, almost black in colour; rich, with a thicker consistency than other types. Pungent but not very salty; it is good for marinating.

japanese soy all-purpose low-sodium soy sauce made with more wheat content than its Chinese counterparts; fermented in barrels and aged. Possibly the best table soy and the one to choose if you only want one variety.

kecap manis a dark, thick, sweet soy sauce. The sweetness is derived from the addition of either molasses or palm sugar when brewed.

light soy fairly thin and, while paler than the others, is the saltiest tasting; used in dishes where the natural colour of the ingredients is to be maintained. Not to be confused with salt-reduced or low-sodium soy sauces.

tamari a thick, dark soy sauce made mainly from soya beans without the wheat used in standard soy sauce.

tomato also known as ketchup or catsup; made from tomatoes, vinegar and spices.

tomato pasta made from a blend of tomatoes, herbs and spices.

worcestershire a dark coloured sauce made from tamarind, molasses, lime, onions, garlic, soy, anchovies, vinegar and seasonings.

SPICES

cinnamon stick dried inner bark of the shoots of the cinnamon tree.

coriander seeds have a mild, lemon-like taste that complements both sweet and savoury dishes. Ground coriander is found in sweet mixed spice blends for cakes and biscuits as well as being used to thicken and flavour curries.

cumin a spice also known as zeera or comino; has a spicy, nutty flavour.

ginger ground or powdered ginger is used as a flavouring in cakes and pies etc; can't be substituted for fresh ginger.

mixed spice a blend of ground spices usually consisting of cinnamon, allspice and nutmeg. star anise the dried star-shaped fruit of a tree native to China. The pods have an astringent aniseed or licorice flavour. Is an essential ingredient in five-spice powder.

sumac a purple-red spice ground from the berries of a small Mediterranean shrub. Adds a tart, lemony flavour.

SUGAR

brown very soft, finely granulated sugar retaining molasses for colour and flavour.

caster also known as superfine or finely granulated table sugar.

white a coarse, granulated table sugar; also known as crystal sugar.

SULTANAS dried grapes; also known as golden raisins.

TAMARI see sauces, soy.

VINEGAR

balsamic made from the juice of Trebbiano grapes; has a deep rich brown colour and a sweet/sour flavour.

balsamic white vinegar (condiment) a clear and lighter version of balsamic vinegar; has a fresh, sweet clean taste.

cider (apple cider) made from the pulp of fermented apples.

raspberry made from fresh raspberries steeped in a white wine vinegar.

red wine based on fermented red wine.

rice a colourless vinegar made from fermented rice and flavoured with sugar and salt. Also known as seasoned rice vinegar.

rice wine made from rice wine lees (sediment left after fermentation), salt and alcohol.

white made from spirit of cane sugar.

white wine made from a blend of white wines.

WALNUTS as well as being a good source of fibre and healthy oils, nuts contain a range of vitamins, minerals and other beneficial plant components called phytochemicals. Each type of nut has a special make-up and walnuts contain the beneficial omega-3 fatty acids.

ZUCCHINI also known as courgette; green, yellow or white vegetable belonging to the squash family.

CONVERSION CHART

MEASURES

One Australian metric measuring cup holds approximately 250ml, one Australian metric tablespoon holds 20ml, one Australian metric teaspoon holds 5ml.

The difference between one country's measuring cups and another's is within a 2- or 3-teaspoon variance, and will not affect your cooking results. North America, New Zealand and the United Kingdom use a 15ml tablespoon. All cup and spoon measurements are level. The most accurate way of measuring dry ingredients is to weigh them. When measuring liquids, use a clear glass or plastic jug with metric markings.

We use large eggs with an average weight of 60g.

DRY MEASURES

METRIC	IMPERIAL
15g	½oz
30g	1oz
60g	2oz
90g	3oz
125g	4oz (¼lb)
155g	5oz
185g	6oz
220g	7oz
250g	8oz (½lb)
280g	9oz
315g	10oz
345g	11oz
375g	12oz (¾lb)
410g	13oz
440g	14oz
470g	15oz
500g	16oz (1lb)
750g	24oz (1½lb)
1kg	32oz (2lb)

LIQUID MEASURES

METRIC	IMPERIAL
30ml	1 fluid oz
60ml	2 fluid oz
100ml	3 fluid oz
125ml	4 fluid oz
150ml	5 fluid oz
190ml	6 fluid oz
250ml	8 fluid oz
300ml	10 fluid oz
500ml	16 fluid oz
600ml	20 fluid oz
1000ml (1 litre)	1¾ pints

LENGTH MEASURES

METRIC	IMPERIAL
3mm	⅛in
6mm	¼in
1cm	½in
2cm	¾in
2.5cm	1in
5cm	2in
6cm	2½in
8cm	3in
10cm	4in
13cm	5in
15cm	6in
18cm	7in
20cm	8in
23cm	9in
25cm	10in
28cm	11in
30cm	12in (1ft)

OVEN TEMPERATURES

These oven temperatures are only a guide for conventional ovens.
For fan-forced ovens, check the manufacturer's manual.

	°C (CELSIUS)	°F (FAHRENHEIT)
Very slow	120	250
Slow	150	275-300
Moderately slow	160	325
Moderate	180	350-375
Moderately hot	200	400
Hot	220	425-450
Very hot	240	475

The imperial measurements used in these recipes are approximate only. Measurements for cake pans are approximate only. Using same-shaped cake pans of a similar size should not affect the outcome of your baking. We measure the inside top of the cake pan to determine sizes.

INDEX

Published in 2012 by ACP Books, Sydney

ACP Books are published by ACP Magazines Limited,
a division of Nine Entertainment Co.

54 Park St, Sydney
GPO Box 4088, Sydney, NSW 2001.

phone (+61)2 9282 8618; fax (+61)2 9126 3702

acpbooks@acpmagazines.com.au; www.acpbooks.com.au

ACP BOOKS

Publishing Director, ACP Magazines · Gerry Reynolds

Publisher · Sally Wright

Editor-in-Chief · Susan Tomnay

Creative Director · Hieu Chi Nguyen

Food Director · Pamela Clark

Published and Distributed in the United Kingdom by Octopus Publishing Group

Endeavour House

189 Shaftesbury Avenue

London WC2H 8JY

United Kingdom

phone (+44)(0)207 632 5400; fax (+44)(0)207 632 5405

info@octopus-publishing.co.uk;

www.octopusbooks.co.uk

Printed by Toppan Printing Co., China

International Foreign Language Rights · Brian Cearnes, ACP Books bcearnes@acpmagazines.com.au

A catalogue record for this book is available from the British Library.

ISBN 9781907428401